I0186025

Impure Thoughts

*

All poems copyright © 2005 - 2012 by JL Cronan.

All design and artwork copyright by Jevon ©, 2012.

                              Anywhere going Nowhere
                                       *

Always I've wanted to go there. I've
          stretched and schemed to get there.
Listened, beseeched, and prayed to get there
          mastered Latin
              read Proust and *Ulysses* to get there
              used sex
              or abstained from sex to get there.
I've drowned myself in seas of whiskey
              dropped LSD
              smoked weed and shot speed to get there.
I've called all day for the tall, fallen girls
              walked the watching dog
              surfed waves of wild roses
              roamed high open spaces
              probed
              prohibited places to get there.
All that going
all that getting there....always going somewhere else
                            always doing the fool
                            bearing down to get there
                            mapping my own third-rate doom.

                                     *

1

Exile poem

Poem 12/19/05
(1)

Twenty-two years ago I first saw you:
    waiting at the Detroit Street bus stop
    on Colfax Avenue.
    (I was on that bus: I'd made my choice weeks earlier).
You came on board, paid your fare and walked down the aisle,
    taking the open seat beside me.

We watched the afternoon streets roll by.
    You wore a glimmery-gold skirt, rather short,
    and silver boots that sparkled and clicked
    with every step you took).

You looked real good, you did,
    coming from heaven as you'd done.
Letting each of us take a long good look,
    wanting to catch your eye.

(A song on someone's radio playing, "Walk On", by Jagger and Tosh)

Many girls have caught my searching eye:
Women who would always stop and stay awhile
I loved them with a boy's stupid, staggering love.
Many girls I've known these last forty years
Now gone
One after another, they all up and walked away
    stayed away
        stayed gone.

The endless night doesn't get it wrong —
Keeps coming along, taking the weak and the strong
So I'll pause, and proclaim while the night's going long:

        Good night to each of you
        You pretty girls all gone
        You, eternal girl
        Sit with me in my broken rocking chair

Maybe some of your silver and gold
Will rub off on me.
And when that last night arrives
Let your perfect love fall all over me.

        ***

Expected
*

In 1951: a long February night
                cloudless
                    moonbright
She can't concentrate on the book she's reading, so
She turns, stretches, and turns off her bedside light.
    She's not to get a good night's sleep
        (not this lovestruck girl on this long cold night)
She's expected to deliver, fast and bloodless, on Valentine's Day
    (already she's four days overdue)

Thursday came with ice and wind,
The nurse hastily switched on the room lights.
They stoked her up with sturdy drugs --
Sufficient, the doctor says, to render the event mostly hidden:
Easy, witless, and smooth as a daydream.

Finally a child breaks forth, wet and red,
With a first burst of newborn voice.
She is not disturbed.
She dreams her way through a baby-blue day.
He is baptized, swaddled, left alone.
For both of them the disturbances arrive later.

***

High School Sex
*

During our senior year in high school the Jesuits invited
Dr. Castle, MD, a gynecologist and Catholic family man, to come
    to our class and give a lecture on sex.
    We were Catholic boys --
    well-taught in the liberal arts and sciences
    but untaught
    in the famous facts of love.
Dr. Castle stepped to the podium on that cold morning in 1968
    and asked us :
    "Is it worth ruining your life for six seconds of pleasure?"
    (Six seconds?)
    A slash of guilt
    cut through me
    but then I laughed it off.
And then came the lecture --
    we got the straight facts
    along with a hard warning to obey
    the rules made law by Paul VI
    or risk losing our eternal souls.
Six seconds -- was Dr. Castle speaking of those godfull moments
    when you feel yourself reaching the edge and sweet victory?
    I claimed
    that reaching the edge takes thousands of seconds
               (gloria ad deliciam)
    lasting as long as you could last.
After the lecture my sarcastic friends started calling me
    'Old Six Seconds'
    and this dayname stuck to me until graduation
    when we all went our separate ways.

She, too, went away ----- childfull,
                    wronged and ruined.
And I just ran and ran and ran
    beaten and sick
    and wrong,
    and did not see her again.

***

Thirty-one Days Later

\-

*

A Humpty-Dumpty kind of fall:
I broke my skull and face
my shoulder and shoulder blade.
Ambulance -- oxygen
I was kept in the ICU for most of a week
 with needles pushed into my arm, leg, and throat.
(I asked about the needle in my throat but have forgotten
 what the nurse said to me.)
Cause of the fall:
my heart got blocked and all went wrong.
I passed out and fell face-first into a sidewalk
while outdoors walking my dog.
Thirty-one days later
I could stand up and begin to get on with it:
walk the local streets, talk with my sons,
navigate beneath the old shuddering stars, watch
everything, read books again, recline and rest,
write long letters, drink cups of deep black coffee,
and move toward the months ahead. Strange --
to stand up and walk on, only to wander into this
out-of-the-way place
where the awful facts can seize your nights
and sear the days.
Watching the world from a fourth-floor window --
the dusty streets lie dead in the afternoon heat
and a thunderstorm rises fast and dark behind the dry
hills and then runs fast and dark away from town.
102 F today... I live in a high western zone and rarely see rain.

Here at the end of the burning day
 I'll take a couple of pills
 to still the crawling pain.
I admit that my hips and knees and other things are going wrong --
 where once I travelled straight and strong (a flesh-and-bone
 man who could run with rhythm and recall all the words

to "Desolation Row") now little remains but thin gristle,
shrinking bone and clouds of doubt.

I've taken three of the comfort pills while reading a poem by Ernest
Dowson, — a poem shaped and held by bright word and phrase
        and claimed by the poet before it was too late.
        Steady verse, though Dowson wasn't: he died early,
        alone, and hard.

I'll read old poems for the rest of the day, drink more coffee
        and take another pill --
        perhaps turn to the bleeding verse of Charlotte Mew.
        She too was finally set free of flesh and bone
                (she drank disinfectant)
        and was swept away into the certain unknown.
Or, there are William Cowper's stormy,
                sacred poems to read --
        for him the days and nights passed with that twisting
                chill within.

I'll find something to do
        something to say --
        I'll write a better poem
        before
        all the right words
        start falling away.

                ***

Deeply Different
*

On a long fall night fraught with teenage dreams he drops his first dose
of LSD at 8:02 pm. Within a hour the room comes alight -- a Persian
carpet brightens in blue and gold and scarlet hues and the easy chair
glows with a pulsing golden light. Shimmering images of the Beatles and
the Who are broken up and fade away from Day-Glo posters tacked to the
room's melting walls...
     His teenage mind will be blown inside-out tonight.
     Seventeen years old and he's reaching for everything now --
     Going beyond thought, beyond all he knows.
                    'have no fear', he tells himself
as he rockets head-first into nameless extravagant worlds.
He's taken beyond the melting room
    past the roof and clouds and sky
    beyond himself and beyond all beyond
    he's reckless, vibrant, and high --
       good-bye   good-bye   good-bye
Ice Cream Frank removes the Steppenwolf LP from the hi-fi player
    and slowly lowers a DOORS record onto the spinning turntable.
Everything goes high, higher, and endless... the music turns into
    vivid storm-bursts of thundering colors that turn again into
    sparkling crystals and swirling stars.
The old sofa gleams in red and purple and green and he can hear a
    rock-and-roll symphony beginning to roar within him...a
    church organ groans and a thousand vibrating rainbows rise
    from the revolving LP...
              a voice chants
           'she comes in colors everywhere'
and all sounds turn into glittering figures of abstract geometry.

Deeply different:
        altered now and here
        there is no he or she or it
        there is no you or I
        nothing becomes everything
        and everything becomes as none
        nowhere is everywhere
        everywhere is nowhere at all
        good-bye   good-bye   good-bye
While colors multiply and divide
      he vanishes
        into the last nowhere dream
    good-bye   good-bye   good-bye

" Key to Infinity " by Jevon© 2012

Playmates and Birds
*

Fifty years ago she shimmied her way out of those long black tights,
hitched up that pinstripe blouse above her shapely waist and
stretched herself out along the low, golden sofa -- she turned
         and gave us a perfect Pepsodent smile.
         I was only a boy back then, but I knew
         a pretty beatnik chick when I saw one.
The camera got her all: Yvette Vickers
                 Playboy's Miss July, 1959.
What was I doing with my summer days in 1959?
         Playing baseball under a clean, roaring sun,
         pitching and catching and running bases
         that shone like peppermint candies

         in the perfect morning light.
         Or, I was shuffling through my thick pack
         of bubble-gum scented baseball cards:
         Nellie Fox, Joe Adcock, Warren Spahn,
         and a couple hundred more -- a stack of
         big-league heroes that required four large
         criss-crossed rubber bands to hold them in place.
(I'm pretty sure they hadn't started hitting me yet.
         Even so, I already knew:
         something's wrong inside of me --
         something as down and deep as mortal sin.).

Forty-five years ago a fortunate man snapped
the sharp centerfold photo of Miss Jo Collins,
soon-to-be- Playmate of the Year, 1964.
         Illuminated in the California night
         she stands beside a glittering swimming pool
         nude but for a loose white shirt and strappy high-heels.
         She's giving us a blue-eyed, satisfied smile.

         I was old enough
             to take a punch, a slap, a crazy blow
             or shed a bit of tainted blood.

In 1964 I was
        playing football in the park
        on Saturday mornings,
        basketball on Friday nights
        acquitting myself honorably on the athletic fields
        of youth.
        Or, I was listening to the Beatles and the Four Seasons,
        singing along with the Beach Boys and reaching falsetto
        but way out of tune...
        Writing love poems
        and finally getting to kiss my girlfriend
        for the first of many times.
By evening's end I'd be holed up
        in my basement bedroom, trying to work through
        all the new thoughts vibrating within.

The camera's eye caught her in mid-stride
        as she walked across the polished stone floor
        wearing a raincoat, long black boots, and nothing more --
Here she comes: Victoria Cunningham
        Miss April, 1975.

By 1975 I was frightened all of the time
        waiting for my life to end, or begin.
        Boozing,
        losing most of my nerves
        pissing time and money away
        going more wrong every day.

Looking at pictures and watching
as scores of lowering blackbirds
gather and wait.

By the Eighties I'd undergone a change:
sober, made amends, even started to pray.
    Married twice more, neither endured,
    nowadays gone back to walking

        and taking my meals alone.

        Reading long novels, seeing none of the latest films,

        remembering those Playmates

        who'd once promised immediate thrills.

Traveling long days on newly cleared trails,
    mindful of the forever blackbirds
    who alight in the brightest places.

        ***

Exile poem
2005

poem 12/14/05

For now (I'm saying so) and evermore
A cold northern blows all day into the night, like
Last night when once again
I walked past your grandfather's old place
(long empty of him, his wife and daughter, and you).

Your nightmares still spirit you away
You fall into the dirty basement dream and you get lost
Below, buried in your grief behind the dream's
Closing door.

As cold and fierce as this lonesome northern blows
As surely as the black winds roar
through this hole in my soul, I know:
I'll not ever be finished with you.

Not ever
In all the nights and days before I'm called away
I'll not ever be finished with you.

***

Her Perfect Hands
*

Regarding the old guy: the one who wrote long poems for her
                          the one who knew all the top girls in town
                          the one who hummed surfing songs, and
                          kissed the girls from up to down...
                          that was more than forty years ago.

History: he tripped and fell, then reached for her ----
         she raised and held him.
         She did all the starting and steering
         as he staggered along the new green streets
         in the quiet parts of their city.
He held on, with a hand and arm around her neck
         (in his other hand he held a fifth of gin).
     I'm a man, he believed...but
     not a chance for him:
     in the end he hurt the girl
     and pissed away most of his God-allotted days.
     He was a bum
     with nowhere to go and little to say.

She finally did let go
her strong and perfect hands dropped this almost-man,
the one who could not stand.

Now, regard the old guy tonight:
        the one who is only watching,
        keening above the darkness
        that rushes across the land.

" El Corazon del Mundo " by Jevon© 2012

Sunday in a High Desert Town

*

We went for breakfast earlier this morning, the watchful guys
    and I. Our topic: God or doom, choose---
        seems easy but isn't always so.
        We meet weekly
            to argue things we think we know.
I'm the God-doubter in our group.
        I'm a doubter who lives in a desert town ---
        leaving my place today, I entered a world
        already ablaze: dry golden light, senseless glare,
        virgin blue.
        Ninety degrees and not yet noon.
Keeping to the shade wherever I can
        I pick up my pace on the way to the cafe
            where all the waitresses are faithfully practicing the English,
        sounding as clear and cool as a rambling stream.
As I arrived the pretty waitress, Rosa,
        crossed in front of me.
        Holding a bowl of green chile, she
        turned
        and gave me a smile like no other I've seen:
        all brown eyes, sparkling lips and teeth.
        For a Sunday moment
        I thought I was seeing the Virgin Mary
        instead of Rose's face.
Esmeralda waits our table today.
        while we talk of ex-wives, seances, and LSD;
        we debate
        how our way can take us beyond the things we know,
        if only to remind ourselves how much work
        we've left to do.
Breakfast over, Esmeralda brought the check.
        As we paid I looked for the sparkling waitress
        but didn't see her anywhere.

While walking home I came upon a grounded bird
    hobbling across the hot concrete.
      Uncertain, I pause,
      pick the bird up and hold it in my hands ---
      torn-up wings.
What to do with a broken bird?
      Kill it quickly so its misery goes fast away?
      Do nothing?
I set the bird down in a shaded place
    and told myself to walk away ---
    back into a day already over but still ablaze.
    Nothing done.
Maybe next Sunday will be cooler
    when we meet again to talk things through ---
    maybe God will show himself
    and I will see things,
    and I will do things,
    and I will be taken beyond the things I know.

                          ****

Her Verity
*

Walking home from the grocery store last night, his once-sturdy
                                    legs showed signs
                                    of decline.
                    It's happened before --
                    you reach a certain stage
                    where things begin to fail:
Knees, hips, wrists, bones, all on their way away...
                    Vanishing days,
                    brain cells failing to spark.
                    Dreams gone astray;
                        unexpected breakdowns of the lungs and heart.
Sometimes things just happen --
                    it comes from somewhere within
                    and carries that ending for him
                    who's on his way home from the store.

Longabout 1963 his adolescent self ceased to be
                what his parents and teachers told him it should be.
By 1973 he'd become a guy who makes a necessary
                    run to the liquor store most every day.
His wife and children were often sad, experts at seething despair.
                    Obedient to booze, he
                    was pretty much an up-for-anything
                                good-for-nothing guy
                                who'd sworn to live life his way:
                                liquor would show him how and why.

The years crawled by...
                    and sometimes things will happen
                    when you keep falling down but cannot die.
He'd been sitting in a yellow lawn chair in a basement kitchen
                (murmuring, drinking Canadian rye whiskey)
                    when his soul broke into hundreds of bleeding pieces.
                    That was the first ending.
Ever since it's been a new story for him.

Last night he saw an ex-girlfriend

                    in a bright and busy coffee shop.
She was sitting at a table by the window and he was passing by outside
                she didn't see him
                    she didn't look up from the book she was reading
                              (<u>Concluding</u>, by Henry Green).
He remembers her coldly-told dirty jokes
                her verity
                and how rare it was to see her smile.
He didn't stop; he kept walking down the avenue
                plodding home
                under a lighted night sky.

Exile poem
2005

Poem 12/17/05
(k)

A hard morning snow falls across Denver town
With a harsh wind that carries the rolling sounds
Of the slowed-down Saturday traffic along Fourteenth Avenue.
              Make your claim, I mumble to myself.
Admission made, stake your claim as the new snow falls
On the morning street.

Last night (I'm telling you)
My best waking thoughts dropped cold and far:
Falling into the nothingness of the coming night.
(By the bedside lamp I had to watch my hands)
I fell asleep around 4:00 a.m., then

Something showed up amidst the nothingness:
I dreamed (in color) about JFK.
He'd arrived, strolling through our neighborhood streets,
He was smiling, his excellent teeth gleaming in the morning light.
He shook my hand,
He shook hands with all of us who'd showed up to welcome him
To our excellent town.
                    Handsome Jack, laughing and smiling
                    Holding the prettiest girls' hands
                    For a moment longer,
                    His eyes holding their eyes another moment longer.

A final flurry of shaking hands,
Smiles, happy-girl sounds, then
The dream dropped away,
disappearing...

I woke up, wondering
At the new day's nothingness
Coming from nowhere.

***

The Ghost Preacher
*

Under the new June sky he strides, bright and crazy,
Pacing the churchyard's shaded places,
Pointing ----
Flapping, and preaching to all those
Who are no longer there.
Nobody left to listen,
Yet he spins and speaks, twisting
His bony shoulders and waving his skinny arms,
Slamming his fist into his burning palm,
Striking at his beating heart,
He testifies
To all the ghosts who've gone away
Disappearing long ago.

All morning he turns to these hidden multitudes
He's the Ghost Preacher: mediating the ridiculous demands
That swarm and swirl around his broken head.
All day he paces and whirls
Proclaiming --
"'All is not well'"
under the white summer sky.

***

Recognizing Her
*

"Existentialism means that nobody can take a bath for you." *
                                    Delmore Schwartz, poet

I used to drink a lot, mainly rye whiskey and beer. My first
wife once told me that I would always smell like a wet bar
rag, no matter how many baths I might take. **

Walking shapes a stance, makes a day -- he's outdoors for the first
    time in weeks, uncertain on his feet. He's wearing the same
    shoes he wore having the heart attack that February morning
    last year.
Coming through the late fall light that comes before the first
    burst of winter chill, he sees a pale dark-haired woman sitting
    on a concrete bench at a bus stop, reading a book. She's wearing
    a black beret and black sweater with a skirt, and long black
    jacket that falls from her shoulders like a loosely wound shroud.
    She holds and turns the book's pages with shapely white hands.
    She looks up at a low gray sky just as a shimmering gloom of
    blackbirds lands nearby. She's reading <u>The Beautiful And Damned</u>.
He wants to stop and say something to this reading woman, recognizing
    her. But he doesn't stop or speak. Anything he might say would
    certainly fall and he'd sound like a strange old man speaking
    strangely to this woman who has not come for him today.
Another damning day is falling away,
    another damning night will take its place.
He walks along the dry, shadowed street,
    a roving ghost
    shaping new soul late in the day.

---

*   "Existentialism: a humanistic philosophy stating that each person
    is responsible for forming his or her own self and must with free
    will oppose the purposeless of one's existence, the hostile
    environment, and the uncertainty of everyday life."
                    The New American Webster Handy College Dictionary (1981)

    ** "I am what I am and that's all I ever can be."
                        Popeye the Sailor

Whaling Days

*

We'd go storming through the darkening Denver streets
    Nineteen Sixty-eight
    Casey, Kosmicki, and I
    private school punks chasing beat thrills in the here and now
    while our chain-smoking public school pal
    John Levi
    held steady at the wheel of his '49 blue-green Jeepster.

Boozed up and downright stoned
        we'd careen headlong into the teenage hipster scene
        shouting Butterfield blues
        we'd roll reckless and free
        like advancing waves on a hurricane sea.
    Casey, Kosmicki, Levi, Bacchus, and I
    nihilists on the loose in the dreaming city
    soaring supersonic with the drugs and Canadian Club rye.

We called these the "whaling days"
        sailing nowhere
        we were small-pond scholars
        gone into dark waters
        pursuing the elusive white whale.

Drinking was my thing ---
        hitting those bottles of pure distilled glory:
        skullbuster rye
          or
        soul-chilling gin
          or
        hundred-proof vodka true
        with Pabst Blue Ribbon for the mornings
        though any strong brew would do.

I was a baseborn fool
        damned by nature to a boozehound's ruin
        dangling in a void
        while
        proferring love-broken poems
        to the girl
        who came as immaculate as a new moon.

I drove a purple Ford Galaxy 500
(a family car my parents allowed me sometimes to use.)
    I was a careful driver always playing it cool
      clicking my turn signal at all the right times
      though it could be trouble knowing left from right
      amidst whiskey dreams
      on those mind-wrecking whaling nights.
Never a crash or a DUI
      the police weren't so vigilant in our whaling days
      as they are now in this post-postmodern age.

Seeking love and ecstasy and coming up empty
    embracing oblivion again and again
    and for long years losing the way...

Sitting in a broken lawn chair in a basement room
    nearly thirty years ago
    with exposed plumbing pipes
    whistling and whooshing and clanking above me
I turned to my left
    and got a stunning glimpse of infinity
    so going that way
    taking steps
    crossing borders
    finally making my way
    into this silent
    shimmering place inside.

Now
looking out my apartment window
    I see aging buses and sparkling cars
    sweeping east and west along Colfax Avenue
    trucks and bicycles and a bright white Cadillac
                   cruise silently by....
I watch for breaking signs of rain
    and see nothing but empty sky.

A beautiful blonde girl in a red miniskirt
    jaywalks across Pennsylvania Street
      a slow old man with a cane plods along
              then stops abruptly
    to study the girl as she glides on by.

Breakneck days and ways are largely done and gone
                                        fallen away
      like cracked bones along a twilighted plain.

Doing some things upright and well, others not...
      day-by-day I'm gaining some know-how
      getting some things dazzling and clear.
      watching
      drinking coffee
Standing up
      as the absence of everything draws near.

****

Ode to the Poe Girl
at the new coffee place
*

Pulling on a washed-up turtleneck and a pair of worn
LL Bean jeans, he leaves his room. Nerves breaking,
debating God: nihil consolora.
He descends eight flights of stairs and leaves the building
where he lives, making his way across the broken and dry
parking lot toward the new coffee place two blocks away.

Taking a chair in a further corner, he sets his cup of coffee
on the tiny table and takes off his leather jacket (ripped up
from taking a dive into a sidewalk while having a heart attack).

    Sitting down at the table he remembers: today
    is All Souls Day.

He sips his coffee and takes a look around the place. His gaze
comes upon a woman at another table who's speaking
to three silent friends.   He's taken by
her narrow, radiant face, long hands and red painted nails.
She's all alight in sudden reds, silver and white.

Thinking about God, watching her: she sips dark tea
from a bright glass cup. She could be the lustrous femme fatale
in a poem by EA Poe (she's all the mystery you'd need).

He's reached the end of a gone-by day.
Having more coffee, thinking about God --
God and women, what can you say?
        (where to tell the troubled mind's tale
          at the end of another day?).
Thinking about God and watching her:
she sparks   then she looks away.

***

Poem 1/02/06
(p)

Way back in my youth-dunked days
Drink and disaster began visiting every day.
Welcome or not they came day after day
and once they'd come,
stayed.

Now I've called myself a **knower**:
A knower 'bout bad luck, sickness, and shame
(drinking my way through the long nights and sunny days).
So when the demons came and took over my mind
   they beat me up
   they beat me down
And then they broke my heart, don't you know?
Never any relief, no,
those whiskey demons gave me no relief
   they broke my head
   they shattered my mind.
No-no-no baby, no...
they gave me no relief, no way.
(trapped as I was in my fatal ways).
They broke my head then shattered my mind,
stomped all over my heart.
   beat me up
   broke me down...
but then, must've been a miracle --

I stood up and got spirited away.
Was a true-life miracle, baby,
how I ever got away.
A true-life miracle:
that's the only way I might explain to you
how I got raised up
  got spirited away.

" The New Universal Man " by Jevon© 2012

Bells
(r)

The great bells began ringing as I walked by the belltower
at Holy Trinity Church.
        A cold wind rushed into me as I rounded the corner.
        Once, I might have paused and thought --
        these bells call for all of us
        morning into night.
        Now I don't think so, though I often think wrong.
A girl and boy stroll along the sidewalk,
        each with an arm around the other's waist.
        Soon, they will have done almost everything with each other.
        Today, they still have a distance to go.
Ducking again into the wind, closing my coat across my chest,
        I walk on by. Perhaps there's more here, and there,
        than meets a watcher's eye.

A woman in my building killed herself yesterday.
        None of us knew her except to nod
        and maybe say hello at the mailboxes each evening.
        She had a nervous smile, and kept her dark hair long;
        did she wonder at the end?
        Did she say anything at all?
Getting through the flash and fade of days I wonder --
        God or not, what to do?
Shutting my eyes I ask which reaches deeper, the yes
        or no of You?

Evening falls into the room.
        I can feel the blackness coming on.
        I'm slumped
        into the corner of an old sofa,
        stretching my arms and legs,
        and then there's You --
        radiant and burning and true.
        I sit up straighter
        but You disappear.

I hear the high bells ringing;
        when they do is that all we will hear -- a last

           stroke of sound
           then nothing more before everything's gone?
           (Perhaps I think wrong)

Tomorrow will go long, again,
and again the night shall go within a moment or two.
           I've been out there and staked my claims --
           I've called for You,
               saying many of your billion names.
Here, then there, You do appear
           but into forever You disappear.
You're everywhere and nowhere
               as I stretch my arms and legs,
               show me how to keep going out there
               and returning here.

                              ***

Old Melodies
*

Towards evening I was reminded of Mary
(while watching a mini-skirted blonde who stood, alone,
in the fiction stacks of the library, browsing
a copy of _Tom Jones_).
With her, the others came gliding along:
girlfriends who'd once held me close in their long and slender arms
when I'd still had parts in some of the boy-meets-girl shows,
when my best efforts to improve would usually end
with all the good women going away (all the wrong ones, too).
I just wasn't any good at well-lit love scenes
though I'd been given most of the best lines.
Women sing
and their songs have run thrills through my blood,
but over is over.

I left the library right before dark, walking away
into October's hard late light,
seeing everything and nothing at once
with reminders of Mary jazzing up my blood.
Memories of the others, too, jumping me up as I moved through
the disappearing light along Thirteenth Avenue.

Unlocking the door at my one bed./bath. place, stepping inside
by the glow of the hallway light,
taking off my hat and hanging up my coat
behind the door
I hear old melodies as I cross the cold linoleum floor:
(hot swing rising from my neighbor's place --- basic
bass beats thumping up through the floor).
I'll get a new pot of coffee going
before the dark comes up behind the cool, starless night.

Under a strong reading light and a cup of coffee with sugar

Dusty Springfield on the record player....
I'll sit in the low green armchair,
first picking up some notes I've left lying there.
Setting the notes to the side,
I'm humming out of tune
when the sound of the night comes into the room.

***

Exile poem

poem 12/30/05
(n)

I think I'll move to Duluth
  (a cold place set beside a cold lake)
I'll leave behind a lifetime's love
Leave all the loves I've failed upon:
        three weddings,
        ~~two sons~~
        three mind-losing breakdowns.

Going away.... I'll take a train
        Glide across the high northern plains
        Roll along the arrow-straight railways
        Arrive in a town that's not heard my name.

I'm thinking of leaving this old and dirty place,
Move to Duluth -- a cold place, a certain change
        of breathing space.
Take myself to this far northern place that waits
By cold, deep lakes.

Forgiveness.... absolution.... redemption
        (all been done, forever so)
Nothing more for me to do or say in this dry, old place...
So, I'll go

To Duluth
I'll watch, and make no harm:
        won't fall in love,
        nor fail on good wives and good sons.
I'll cease running, walk quietly and take it slow,
Sit by the lake's green shores and do no harm.
This I shall do once I've arrived in Duluth.

✶

" Is Spring coming or has Autumn gone? " by Jevon© 2012

How About It?
A **Suicide**-By-God Prayer

Bestow that lasting holiday:
grant me release, finally.
Let come the finisher, doom,
that stirs behind the door to this room.
Rest me.

Long have I known nothing
while running along the edges
in this one-man room:
inviting the void
but getting my own voice
thrown back at me.

How about it, God?
Break me away from this do-and-die show,
give me the bum's rush right out of this world.
Deliver me to a place
where all I must do is ---- **do nothing**.
Declare my absence.
Cite "natural causes",
And when judgment day comes marauding along?
Remember some of the right things done in Your name.